I0446299

Negotiating for Beginners 2024

Unleashing Powerful Strategies for Winning with Ease – A Practical Guide to Successful Deal Making"

By

Daryl V. Meyer

Copyright page

About the Author

Meet Daryl V. Meyer, a seasoned professional with a significant energy for business and money matters. As the creative force behind this guide, Daryl V. Meyer brings an abundance of involvement and bits of knowledge gathered from years drenched in the unique domains of business and money.

Daryl V. Meyer has carved a niche for himself in the business world, having navigated the complexities of various industries with a keen eye for financial strategies and negotiations. His excursion in the business scene has leveled up his abilities as well as filled a profound obligation to sharing information and enabling others to succeed in the monetary space.

With a finger on the beat of the consistently developing business scene, Daryl V. Meyer is aware of the difficulties people encounter when examining financial issues. His comprehension interfaces past the speculative as he organizes veritable encounters and viable snippets of data into the pages of this aide, making it a significant asset for perusers hoping to manage their monetary insight.

Notwithstanding his obligation to composing, Daryl V. Meyer has committed to the business and financial field through Little Shift, Lasting Impact and Crafting a Stress-Resilient Life. This sets his believability as well as positions him as a confided in expert for those looking for direction in the domains of business and money.

As readers delve into the pages penned by Daryl V. Meyer they embark on a journey guided by someone who not only understands the intricacies of business and finance but who is genuinely passionate about sharing this knowledge. Whether you are a seasoned professional hoping to refine your monetary methodologies or a hopeful business person venturing into the business world, Daryl V Meyer's bits of knowledge give a guide to outcome in the unique convergence of business and money.

Table of content

Introduction

Welcome to "Negotiating for Beginners," this is your critical asset for prevailing at making negotiations. In this present reality where magnificent correspondence and critical abilities to think are fundamental, the capacity to effectively deal is an esteemed benefit.This book is expected to outfit you with the data and capacities you truly need to deal conveniently and obtain great outcomes, whether you're administering capable endeavors, social associations, or normal issues.

We shall go on a journey to deconstruct the complexities of bargaining in the following chapters.This book is planned for beginners, with each step ensuring clearness and straightforwardness. You will acquire a superior comprehension of arranging ideas and have the option to set them in motion with the help of functional experiences, models from this present reality, and bit by bit guidelines.

Every part is intended to progressively further develop your discussion abilities, from getting a handle on the essentials of compelling correspondence to perceiving partners and making clear goals.We will examine the subtleties of negotiation and give you devices for defeating hindrances, adjusting to various circumstances, and exploring intricacies.

A methodical approach to both pre-negotiating preparation and successful negotiation execution is provided by this book's step-by-step recommendations.Whether you're a novice or expecting to step up your abilities to organize, these helpers will be splendid resources for extending your sureness and dominance.

Recall that learning is a reliable participation as we research the specialty of putting together.The last segment urges you to consider your discussions and underlines the probability that each obligation gives you a significant chance to progress.

Are you willing to start on a path to become a skilled negotiator? Let's get started and discover the keys to negotiating for success and beyond.

Chapter 1: Brief overview of negotiation and its significance

Negotiation is a discourse between at least two gatherings determined to arrive at a commonly valuable result or settling a contention. In exchange, each party will attempt to convince the other one to concur with their perspective. The objective is to keep away from contentions and questions and arrive at some type of give and take between parties.

It also can involve two or more parties working together to achieve a goal that all parties can agree on. One party will put its situation ahead, while the other will either acknowledge the circumstances introduced or counter with its own situation. The interaction goes on until the two players consent to a goal or exchange server without one.

Negotiating is applied in numerous parts of daily existence, despite the fact that you may not understand it. Negotiating a price on the open market, negotiating a car purchase at a dealership, negotiating compensation or a job, and negotiating between warring nations are some examples from everyday life.

Experienced mediators will frequently attempt to advance however much as could be expected about the other party's situation before a discussion starts, including what the qualities and shortcomings of that position are, the manner by which to get ready to protect their positions, and any counter-contentions the other party will probably make.

In capable settings, conversation expects a fundamental part in business deals, work agreements, and key associations. It is the basic piece of practical work with tries, empowering people and relationships to change their propensities, resolve clashes, and stimulate potential affiliations. Ruling negotiation capacities is an indication of convincing drive and an imperative driver of various leveled accomplishments.

Past the meeting room, Negotiation is woven into the texture of our day to day routines. From settling on family matters to exploring social elements, the capacity to arrange enables people to verbalize their necessities, figure out the points of view of others, and manufacture arrangements that maintain common regard.

In this part, we will relax the layers of exchange, analyzing its different plans and uncovering information into its striking power.Remember that discussion is something other than an expertise as we examine the complexities; Beyond individual transactions, it's a strategic way of thinking and solving problems. It is an instrument for strengthening, joint effort, and eventually, accomplishing results that endure for an extremely long period. Oblige us as we set out on this journey to demystify conversation and outfit you with the data and capacities to investigate its complexities with conviction and cunning.

Importance of negotiation in various aspects of life

The act of negotiation, which is frequently alluded to as the specialty of accomplishing results that the two players are content with, reaches out past corporate meeting rooms and into the complex texture of our regular day to day existences. Here, the multi-layered significance of exchange is uncovered, displaying its unavoidable effect on proficient development, relational connections, compromise, and, surprisingly, the standard choices that shape our ordinary presence.

• **Progression in one's career:**

In the expert field, negotiation isn't simply an ability; an essential device can impel vocations higher than ever. The capacity to haggle successfully during pay conversations, project joint efforts, or legally binding arrangements is a distinctive component. individuals are drawn in to advocate for their worth, makes satisfying work environments, and positions them as strong trailblazers prepared for driving real accomplishment.

• Business and Exchange:

Negotiation is the beating heart of trade and business transactions in the powerful scene.Whether it's getting an agreement, shaping key organizations, or exploring complex legally binding arrangements, powerful discussion is vital. It goes beyond just making deals; discussion is the foundation of building getting through business connections, improving seriousness, and getting competitive edges in the steadily advancing commercial center.

• Relationships with others:

The effect of negotiation resonates into the domain of individual connections. From familial elements to kinships and heartfelt organizations negotiation is basic to cultivating understanding and agreement. Constructive discussion is also encouraged by it, encourages conflict resolution, and encourages individuals to investigate the specifics of shared liabilities. The ability to orchestrate supports the securities that structure the basis of adaptable and fulfilling affiliations.

• Compromise:

In our current reality where clashes are unavoidable, negotiation arises as a strong instrument for goal. Parties are provided with a structured framework within which they can voice their grievances, comprehend the perspectives of others, and collaborate on finding solutions. Whether in networks, working environments, or on a worldwide scale, exchange fills in as a foundation for relieving pressures and adding to cultural congruity.

• **Ordinary Navigation:**

Our day-to-day lives are subtly woven with negotiation, influencing the choices we regularly make. A person's preferences, values, and priorities are reflected in their negotiations, which can include deciding where to eat with friends or delegating household duties. These apparently unremarkable talks aggregately add to forming the surface of our everyday schedules and social connections.

This part lays the structure for considering business as a monstrous power that overshadows our own and skilled scenes instead of as a desolate matchless quality. Evaluating the general effect of the debate is basic. The intricacies of trade will be covered through and through in coming about areas, giving you the data and resources vital to accept its prizes in different settings.

Common misconceptions about negotiation

Common misconceptions that frequently obscure this dynamic process must be confronted and dispelled in order to unravel the complex world of negotiation. These disarrays, laid out in dreams and misinterpretations, can baffle individuals from grasping the greatest limit of their conversation capacities. This part fills in as a compass, directing us through the obscurity of normal doubts encompassing exchange.

• **Win-Lose Mentality**:

One prevailing misconception is the idea that negotiation is inherently a win-lose scenario, where one party's gain is directly proportionate to the other's loss. As a general rule, viable discussion looks to make an incentive for all gatherings included, encouraging a mutually beneficial result. It's anything but a lose situation; rather, it's a collaboration to fulfill various interests.

• Solely Transactional:

Another common misperception is viewing negotiation as a purely transactional exchange, confined to business deals and financial transactions. In truth, exchange is an undeniable mastery that loosens up past the master area. It shapes individual affiliations, resolves clashes, and impacts standard course. Seeing its extensive property is basic to harnessing its notable power.

• Only for Extroverts:

There's a prevalent notion that effective negotiators must be inherently extroverted, charismatic individuals. This erroneous interpretation overlooks the numerous exchange styles. Introverts, armed with strong analytical and listening skills, often excel in negotiation. Success lies in flexibility and using individual characteristics, not acclimating to speculations.

• Limited to Formal Settings:

Negotiation is not confined to formal conference rooms or business . It can occur in loosened up conversations or during family route.The affirmation that exchange is a critical piece of standard normal presence fosters its endorsement and underlines its significance in different settings.

• Quick Fix Solutions:

Contrary to a common misconception, negotiation is not always about finding quick-fix solutions. A cycle needs key reasoning, undivided attention, and smart preparation. Surged arrangements might prompt subpar results. Persistence and a far reaching comprehension of the discussion scene are necessary to progress.

• **Always Contentious:**

While conflict is inherent in some negotiations, assuming that all negotiations are inherently contentious is a misconception. Talented mediators focus on joint effort, looking for shared belief and understanding to genially agree. The capacity to transform possible struggles into open doors for common increase is a sign of viable discussion.

As we investigate the parts ahead, it is influential to disperse these off track decisions, taking into account an all the more clear understanding of conversation's different nature. The path is cleared for a more nuanced and powerful method for managing negotiation in both master and individual settings by testing these legends.

Chapter 2: The Basics of Effective Communication

More is required than just exchanging information when it comes to making effective communication. It is important to understand the emotion and purpose underlying the information. In addition to being able to properly deliver a message, you must also be able to listen in such a manner that you grasp the whole meaning of what is being said and make the other person feel heard and understood.

Effective communication appears to be innate. Be that as it may, all too regularly, something turns out badly when we attempt to interact with others. We say one thing, but the other person hears something completely different, resulting in misunderstandings, dissatisfaction, and conflict.This could upset your connections at home, school, and work.

Communicating more simply and effectively will require many people to learn new skills. Acquiring these abilities might extend your connections to other people, lay out more trust and regard, and upgrade participation, critical thinking, and your overall social and close to home wellbeing, whether you're expecting better correspondence with your life partner, children, business, or colleagues.

Negotiating progress depends on developing a strong correspondence. This part inspects the fundamentals of correspondence, enlightening the cutoff points and techniques that go probably as the establishment for gigantic and strong affiliations.

• **Learn to be a good listener.**

When talking with people, we often concentrate on what we should say. Effective communication, on the other hand, is less about talking and more about listening. Listening correctly is not just comprehending the words or information being delivered, but also comprehending the feelings the speaker is attempting to express.

There is a significant distinction between attentive listening and just hearing. When you really listen—when you are engaged with what's being said—you will take note of minor intonations in someone's voice that indicate how that person is feeling and the emotions they're attempting to transmit. When you actively pay attention, you not only better understand the other person, but you also make that other feel heard and understood, which may help you form a stronger, deeper relationship.

You will also go through a process that helps you feel better physically and emotionally and reduces stress by connecting in this way. If the person you're speaking with is calm, for example, listening attentively will assist to calm you as well. Similarly, if the individual is upset, you might assist calm them down by listening carefully and making them feel understood.

• Communication through speech

Verbal communication is the skill of efficiently conveying your thoughts, feelings, and ideas using words and language. A fundamental limit is huge in various highlights of life. Communicating verbally will help you in redesigning your social capacities in both individual and master settings. You can also perform well in public speaking activities.

The foundation of good verbal communication is speaking clearly and intentionally. The manner in which you articulate your thoughts might affect how your message is gotten and deciphered. You must do the following to do this:

- Take special note of how you pronounce each word.

- Improvement in your expression could be achieved through pronunciation exercises.

- Set a reasonable speed for your discourse. Speaking too rapidly might make it difficult to understand, while speaking too slowly can cause boredom.

- Pauses should be deliberately placed. Important points can be brought to light during pauses. Pauses will also enable you to give your audience time to assimilate information or to organize your thoughts.

- Upgrade your vocabulary by learning new words. The training will assist you with articulating your thoughts all the more plainly and articulately.

Knowing how to change your pitch and tone Is another important thing. Pitch and tone of your voice are useful assets for communicating your sentiments and framing associations with the individuals who are listening to you. To communicate effectively verbally, you must adapt your tone and pitch to the discussion or presentation's context and objective.

• **Be succinct.**

Conciseness in communication refers to the capacity to deliver your message clearly and concisely. It is usually preferable to organize your ideas before speaking or writing. This is due to the fact that clear thinking always leads to increased communication and production.

When talking with someone, you should use straightforward, unambiguous language. The objective here is to guarantee that your message is simply comprehended rather than to wow with intricacy.

Thus, it is basic to try not to utilize superfluous words and material that might cloud your message.

Most importantly, each word you utter ought to add to the nature of your discussion.

• **Be specific and concise.**

Another ability you ought to create to turn into an effective communicator is the capacity to be precise and clear with your message. On the off chance that you are the sort of individual who gives an unauthentic history with no proof to back it up, you are not a decent communicator.

Your audience will understand you better if you are particular with your message. Being explicit with your message additionally involves offering points of interest in regards to the data you're conveying, like measurements and numbers.

Moreover, you ought to be unambiguous in your articulation. You believe your message should be distinct and clear so that individuals can fathom you rapidly. Clarity in a message is critical since it guarantees that every member of the work team understands you without difficulty. To be clear in your communication, use basic terminology, speak in an energetic voice, and state your aims clearly. It likewise helps on the off chance that you can impart in a similar language as your crowd. You may now use innovation to concentrate on Spanish, French, German, and other unknown dialects quicker.

• Nonverbal communication is essential.

Your non-verbal communication is basic to your capacity to actually impart. Your tone, eye to eye connection, facial feelings, and hand signals are more fundamental than your words. Hand motions when communicating show that you are self-assured and bold. As a result, it permits the individual with whom you are conversing to pay attention to you and genuinely listen to what you are saying.

While speaking, using nonverbal communication may help you create deeper relationships with others and communicate your message more simply and efficiently. Find out about different hand signals, tones, and positions to better your nonverbal correspondence. Additionally, focus on others' non-verbal communication to all the more likely handle the message.

• Self-assurance

Communication assertiveness is the capacity to convey your demands, opinions, and feelings boldly and politely. Explore different avenues regarding using "I" expressions to convey your thoughts and feelings. Say something like, "I believe this approach is more effective" rather than "This approach is better."

Furthermore, throughout your discussion, you should retain a forceful yet courteous tone. Assertiveness should not be confused with hostility. It is because it is a clear and consistent statement of your point of view.

When required, you must be able to argue your points of view respectfully. It is critical to never be afraid to speak up for what you believe in, even if it means addressing disputes or confrontations.

• Be at ease.

Anxiety and stress may stifle communication and discourage you. Both of these factors might make you an unsuccessful communicator. You should be relaxed and stress-free in order to converse properly. Stress leads you to select the incorrect collection of words. It makes it more challenging for your audience members to get a handle on what you're talking about

Also, being cool and stress-free throughout a conversation allows you to better comprehend the essence of the discourse. It additionally permits you to choose among battle and flight modes. Depending on the scenario, fight or flight implies to respond or remain silent.

Moreover, being quiet ensures that you make decisions that you won't lament from now on and that you stay away from different issues. As a result, being cool is advised in order to communicate successfully.

• Educate

To be a successful communicator, you should enlighten your audience on the topic of your conversation. It would give your listeners a rough notion of what was going on. It would likewise make it more straightforward for understudies to understand the information. Aside from that, you should tell those listening about the main aspects or topics that they should pay attention to and remember during the talk.

Educating individuals on the subject regarding the discussion readies your crowd and permits them to make the necessary move to figure out you. You should also clarify your views in depth to your audience, as not everyone will have the same level of knowledge as you. Making sense of your thoughts and perspectives exhaustively helps many individuals in the crowd, permitting you to be a phenomenal communicator.

• Flexibility

Adaptability in communication is tailoring your communication style to the context and persons involved. You may likewise work on your flexibility in correspondence through various methods. Considering the following suggestions can undoubtedly assist you in this regard:

Always pay great attention to other people's preferences and communication methods. Understanding your audience's specific wants and expectations is the first step towards adaptability.

Adapt your communication strategy as needed. It implies that you should change your message to a fluctuated populace, people with varying characters, or different hierarchical designs. Moreover, you ought to be available to include and be ready to make changes.

Generally speaking, adaptability is a persistent cycle, and having the option to further develop your correspondence style is a critical ability all by itself.. As a result, it is always critical to take feedback constructively and enhance your adaptation abilities in order to express your message as effectively as possible.

• **Use visuals**

Representing the information you want to provide your audience in a visual style allows people to remember it for a long period. It is ingrained in human nature that we digest information far faster than it is conveyed in the form of graphics. As per one review, people have an extended capacity to fathom and hold pictures after some time.

In line with the same study, we do not recall words for a longer period of time than we do visuals. As a result, in order to be a good communicator, you must have the ability to make your arguments received by your audience, and it is recommended that you use appropriate information-delivery tactics, such as visual communication. Visual correspondence is the portrayal of data as outlines, guides, photos, and diagrams.

• **Demonstrate empathy**

Empathy is synonymous with comprehension. There will be occasions when your statements or ideas conflict those of other team members or members. However, you should not be furious or frustrated in this scenario. All things being equal, appreciate their perspective and hail their boldness. Consider it healthy competition.

Use comments like "I know what you're trying to say, but..." or "Sorry, but I think..." to demonstrate superior comprehension and ensure that others regard you as a competitive communicator. Statements like this will make people aware that you were interested in their opinions and that would increase their spirits.

• Telling stories

Storytelling is often regarded as one of particularly crucial communication abilities for engaging and persuading others. When it comes to studying storytelling for better and more interesting communication, there are several factors to consider.

For instance, you should write a story with a distinct beginning, middle, and finish. Structure your story to draw in the crowd and effectively express your point. Use simple words and images to construct a mental representation for your audience. It will help you in drawing in their faculties and feelings to make your story extraordinary.

You ought to likewise work on narrating in various settings. Narrating is a different ability that might be improved over the long haul, whether for corporate introductions, individual stories, or promoting drives. You should continue to practice in order to develop your narrative ability.

• **Completion**

Completing your phrases while talking is what completeness entails. On occasion, you may observe that folks begin a phrase. However, after a little time, they get so perplexed that they begin discussing other issues while abandoning the original. Accordingly, every one of these creates outrageous turmoil and upsets effective correspondence.

To communicate successfully, you must thoroughly clarify the first point before moving on to the next. Also, make certain that you clarify your ideas in a logical order, and that there is a link and rational deduction within the phrases.

Furthermore, it is critical when responding to someone, since completeness makes many things in communication easy and orderly. Thus, to be a great communicator, you should rehearse this ability.

• Debate Goal

Compromise is the expertise of effectively overseeing and settling issues in different circumstances, like individual connections, organizations, or local area collaborations. Learning compromise strategies might be valuable in both expert and individual circumstances.

Open correspondence can advance sincere talk. Effective conflict resolution necessitates the creation of a secure environment in which all parties feel heard and appreciated, making it easier to unearth underlying issues.

As a result, in order to develop conflict resolution as part of your ability to communicate, you must do the following:

Maintain your composure and cool amid confrontations. The ability to understand people on a deeper level is basic in overseeing tough spots.

You must guarantee that you hear both sides of the story. Seeing every one of sides' perspectives is basic for laying out agreement and settling any conflict genially and successfully.

Besides, instead of pursuing individual achievement, it centers around tracking down commonly useful arrangements. Positive connections and team dynamics are fostered by win-win solutions in dispute resolution.

• **Provide and Accept Feedback**

Giving and accepting feedback is a key skill for good communication. Giving input spurs individuals, while getting criticism permits you to recognize and fix your imperfections.

You may not receive all of the compliments on your character. They may be challenging to pursue on occasion, yet you should answer them decisively to be a superior communicator. Additionally, endeavor to get a handle on the issues that are driving people to give remarks. If you don't understand what the feedback implies, you can always ask the senders.

• **Cultural Awareness**

Cultural sensitivity is concerned with being aware of and respecting the values and standards of society of others. When communicating, you must be attentive to the cultural values of others. Here are a few functional ideas for adjusting to social responsiveness:

You ought to find out about assorted societies and practices. Focus profoundly on learning about various networks' accounts, customs, and convictions.

Make no judgements or preconceptions based on cultural differences. Recall that every individual is interesting, and wide speculations can prompt distortion and offense.

Above all, it is preferable to keep a willingness to listen and a readiness to learn from others with different ideas. Engaging in cross-cultural contacts and exploring opportunities to improve your awareness of various cultures can also be beneficial in this situation.

• **Use your time-sensitive approach.**

You have to understand your team members in order to interact successfully at work or in your career. So, instead of sitting alone and eating during your coffee or lunch break, make the most of it. Utilize that chance to look into your collaborators and have more profound information on them.

The further comprehension you might interpret individuals in your group, the better you will be equipped for speaking with them.

Rehearsing these capacities can permit you to convey all the more effectively with others.

Understanding the role of communication in negotiation

Communication remains as the backbone of negotiation, molding the elements, results, and generally speaking outcome of the interaction. This section seals with the confounded trade among correspondence and conversation, loosening up its dire work in delivering critical affiliations and driving discussions towards great objectives.

• Information Exchange:

At its core, communication in negotiation serves as a conduit for the exchange of information. It's a powerful interaction where each party conveys their points of view, interests, and needs. An indisputable and clear movement of information establishes the groundwork for informed bearing and mutual perspective.

• Building Trust and Rapport:

Effective communication fosters trust and rapport between negotiating parties. Straightforward and open correspondence makes an air of legitimacy, moderating doubt and improving the probability of cooperation. Trust is the bedrock whereupon effective exchanges are constructed.

• Clarifying Expectations:

Communication is instrumental in clarifying expectations. Mediators articulate their objectives, targets, and wanted results, guaranteeing a mutual perspective between all gatherings included. This clearness limits blunders and changes suppositions, clearing a path for a more significant trade process.

• Managing Conflict:

In negotiations, conflicts are inevitable. Communication fills in as a device for overseeing and settling these contentions usefully. Talented arbitrators proficiently explore conflicts through viable correspondence, looking for shared conviction and changing likely barricades into open doors to split the difference.

• Emphasizing Interpersonal Relationships:

Beyond the transactional aspects, communication in negotiation emphasizes the interpersonal relationships between parties. It includes grasping the feelings, inspirations, and individual points of view that shape the exchange scene. Building associations on a human level adds to a more cooperative and positive discussion climate.

• Strategic Messaging:

Communication in negotiation is strategic. Negotiators cautiously make their messages to impact insights, oversee assumptions, and guide the heading of the exchange. Vital correspondence includes thinking about the timing, content, and conveyance of messages to boost influence and accomplish wanted results.

• Active Problem-Solving:

Effective communication propels active problem-solving. It urges gatherings to investigate arrangements, conceptualize choices, and participate in cooperative work to address difficulties. The trading of thoughts and points of view makes for inventive and commonly gainful arrangements.

Understanding the job of correspondence in discussion goes past excelling at passing on data; it involves perceiving correspondence as a unique power that shapes connections, settles clashes, and eventually drives the exchange cycle towards progress. As we explore through this section, how about we unwind the complexities of correspondence's impact on discussion and furnish ourselves with the abilities to impart successfully in different arranging situations.

Verbal and non-verbal communication skills

Effective communication in negotiation loosens up to be sure alone, wrapping both verbal and non-verbal points of view. It researches the nuanced relationship of verbal and non-verbal social cutoff points, uncovering understanding into how authority of the two adds to helpful discussions.

Verbal Communication Skills:

• Clarity and Precision:

Articulating thoughts and intentions with clarity avoids misunderstandings. Accuracy in verbal enunciation works on the likelihood of common point of view and productive trade results.

• **Active Listening**

The ability to really listen is a fundamental verbal mastery. It involves not only hearing but comprehending and responding thoughtfully to the information shared by the other party. Undivided attention cultivates a cooperative climate and shows real commitment.

• **Effective Questioning:**

Crafting insightful and open-ended questions is a skill that deepens understanding.Questioning strategically prompts the other party to share more data, giving important bits of knowledge to informed direction.

• **Empathy in Verbal Expression**:

Showing empathy through words establishes a connection. Verbal acknowledgment of the other party's concerns or emotions demonstrates a willingness to understand and collaborate, fostering a positive negotiation environment.

• Negotiation Vocabulary:

Developing a negotiation-specific vocabulary enhances communication effectiveness. Making Use of terms that resonate within the negotiation context contributes to clearer communication and aligns parties on key concepts.

Non-Verbal Communication Skills:

• Body Language:

Body language conveys unspoken messages. A negotiator's stance, signals, and looks can impact discernments. Adjusting non-verbal signs to verbal messages constructs trust and credibility.

• Eye Contact:

Maintaining appropriate eye contact signals attentiveness and confidence. It achieves an association among moderators and conveys truthfulness. However, excessive or insufficient eye contact may convey different messages.

• Facial Expressions:

Facial expressions reveal emotions and intentions. A genuine and congruent facial expression enhances trust, while inconsistencies between verbal and facial cues may raise suspicion.

• Gestures:

Thoughtful use of gestures complements verbal communication. Very much coordinated and fitting motions underscore central issues and add to a dynamic and connecting with negotiation environment.

• Proxemics:

Proxemics, or the use of personal space, influences interpersonal dynamics.

Understanding and regarding social standards in regards to individual space is critical for successful non-verbal correspondence.

• Voice Tone and Pitch:

Variations in voice tone and pitch convey emotions and emphasize certain points. A controlled and modulated voice contributes to a persuasive and authoritative communication style.

In ruling both verbal and non-verbal social capacities, arbitrators work on their ability to pass on messages, develop similarity, and investigate the intricacies of conversation actually. As we dig into the ensuing sections, we should keep refining these abilities to impart actually in different negotiating situations.

Active listening techniques

Effective negotiation relies on the expertise of undivided attention, a unique cycle that goes past simply hearing words. This goes over into full focus techniques, focusing on their significance in empowering normal appreciation and preparing for viable conversation results.

• Give Full Attention:

The foundation of active listening is providing undivided attention to the speaker. Minimize distractions, focus on the speaker, and refrain from formulating responses while listening. It creates a space for genuine engagement.

• Maintain Eye Contact:

Sustaining appropriate eye contact conveys attentiveness and interest. It lays out an association with the speaker and signs that their words are esteemed. Notwithstanding, it's essential to adjust eye to eye connection to keep away from uneasiness.

• Use Verbal Affirmations:

Employ verbal cues, such as nodding or using affirming statements, to signal active engagement. These certifications promise the speaker that their message is being gotten and urge them to share all the more transparently.

• Paraphrase and Summarize:

Periodically paraphrase or summarize the speaker's points to confirm understanding. This shows undivided attention as well as gives a chance to explain any expected misinterpretations.

• Ask Clarifying Questions:

Seeking clarification through well-crafted questions shows a commitment to understanding. Clarifying questions not only elicit additional information but also convey a genuine interest in the speaker's perspective.

• Reflect Emotions:

Acknowledge and reflect the emotions expressed by the speaker. This includes perceiving both verbal and non-verbal signals connected with feelings. Reflecting feelings cultivates a more profound association and understanding.

• Avoid Interrupting:

Resisting the urge to interrupt allows the speaker to express their thoughts fully. Interferences can disturb the progression of communication and block the speaker's capacity to really pass on their message.

• Practice Empathy:

Build empathy by putting yourself in the shoes of the speaker. Figure out their point of view, feelings, and fundamental inspirations. Exhibiting compassion upgrades compatibility and adds to a cooperative exchange climate.

• Suspend Judgment:

Withhold judgment and preconceived notions while listening. Embracing a liberal methodology takes into consideration a more goal comprehension of the speaker's perspective, regardless of whether it varies from your own.

• Respond Appropriately:

Smart reactions exhibit undivided attention. Make reactions that recognize the speaker's message and add to the continuous discourse. Avoiding knee-jerk reactions promotes a constructive exchange of ideas.

Active listening is an expertise that changes negotiation elements, preparing for shared understanding and joint effort. As we progress through this investigation of communication in negotiation, consolidating these undivided attention procedures will improve your capacity to connect genuinely with others and explore negotiation with finesse.

Chapter 3: Identifying Stakeholders and Their Interests

In the complex dance of negotiation, understanding the scene of stakeholders and their inclinations is similar to exploring a diverse chessboard. Here, the part investigates the tremendous course of seeing accomplices and disentangling their propensities, an imperative stage in making a useful negotiation system.

• Recognizing Key Players:

The first step is to identify all relevant stakeholders. These are individuals or groups directly or indirectly impacted by the negotiation outcome. Key players might include leaders, powerhouses, or those with a personal stake in the negotiation's ramifications.

Delve into the interests and motivations of each stakeholder. What are their fundamental objectives, concerns, and needs? A complete comprehension of these variables lays the foundation for fitting negotiation moves toward that resound with every stakeholder.

• **Conducting Stakeholder Mapping:**

Create a stakeholder map to visualize relationships and power dynamics. This tool helps in categorizing stakeholders in light of their impact and interest in the negotiation. Stakeholder mapping gives experiences into expected coalitions and areas of conflict.

• **Considering Internal and External Stakeholders:**

Acknowledge both internal and external stakeholders. Internal stakeholders might incorporate colleagues, the executives, or representatives, while external stakeholders include clients, providers, administrative bodies, and the more extensive local area. Each gathering carries unmistakable interests to the exchange table.

• Significance of Empathy

Empathy has a huge impact in perceiving different associates and choosing their penchants. Come at the situation as indicated by their perspective, seeing the viewpoints, concerns, and goals that drive every accessory. This empathetic strategy shapes the support for persuading assistant obligation.

• Stakeholder Interviews and Surveys:

Engage stakeholders through interviews or surveys to gather insights directly. This proactive methodology gives significant data as well as signs a promise to inclusivity and a cooperative negotiation process.

• Assessing Influence and Power Dynamics:

Evaluate the influence and power dynamics among stakeholders. Distinguish those with dynamic power and the individuals who might influence suppositions. Perceiving the elements assists in forming systems that line up with the overarching power structures.

• Prioritizing Stakeholder Interests:

Prioritize stakeholders based on the significance of their interests to the negotiation's success. Understanding which interests are non-debatable and which can be exchanged or compromised helps with key decision-production during the negotiation cycle.

• Anticipating Hidden Stakeholders:

Be vigilant for hidden or unforeseen stakeholders who may emerge during the negotiation. These could be individuals or groups not initially apparent but hold sway over critical aspects. Expecting these elements limits astonishments and upgrades discussion versatility.

• Consistent Perception and adaptability:

Stakeholder dynamics evolve, requiring continuous monitoring. Regularly reassess the landscape, considering changes in interests, power structures, and external factors. Flexibility guarantees that exchange systems stay pertinent and receptive to dynamic partner situations.

Turning into the best at recognizing accomplices and deciphering their tendencies is an establishment in the conversation cycle. As we investigate through this part, remember that accessories are dynamic parts, and a nuanced impression of their propensities is head for planning negotiation toward useful and typically beneficial results.

Recognizing key players in a negotiation

In the mind boggling dance of exchange, perceiving the central members is much the same as recognizing the directors of a symphonic exhibition. This part jumps into the basic course of seeing focal individuals in an exchange, explaining the critical work they play in embellishment results and coordinating the negotiation cycle.

• Decision-Makers:

Identify those wielding decision-making authority. These are the people with the capacity to greenlight arrangements and shape a definitive direction of the negotiation. Seeing pioneers is central for focusing on strong figures.

• Influencers:

Influencers may not hold formal decision-making power but can sway opinions and outcomes. People like these frequently have skill, magnetism, or an organization of connections that make their points of view effective. Recognizing powerhouses is vital to grasping expected roads of help or obstruction.

• Subject Matter Experts:

In complex negotiations, subject matter experts bring specialized knowledge to the table. Perceiving and including these people guarantees an exhaustive comprehension of specialized viewpoints and works with informed independent direction.

• Legal Advisors:

The Legal advisors play a critical role in negotiations, guiding parties on legal implications and ensuring compliance.

Identifying and consulting with legal experts early in the process helps navigate potential legal challenges and reinforces the negotiation's foundation.

• Internal Stakeholders:

Look within your organization for internal stakeholders. Colleagues, office heads, and chiefs might have a personal stake in the negotiation's prosperity. Perceiving the jobs of inner partners encourages attachment and guarantees arrangement with authoritative objectives.

• External Stakeholders:

Beyond the internal realm, external stakeholders such as clients, suppliers, and regulatory bodies exert influence. Perceiving their importance is fundamental for expecting outer elements that might affect the negotiation interaction and results.

• Decision-Influencing Teams:

In some negotiations, decisions are collective and influenced by teams rather than individuals. Distinguishing central members inside choice impacting groups guarantees a nuanced comprehension of overall vibes and empowers designated commitment.

• Gatekeepers:

Gatekeepers control access to decision-makers and information. Perceiving these people and developing positive associations with them can work with smoother correspondence and improve the negotiation cycle.

• Unofficial Decision-Makers:

In certain scenarios, unofficial decision-makers may hold sway. These people might not have a conventional title however have a huge impact. Perceiving their job is indispensable for grasping the full range of force elements at play.

• Emerging Leaders:

Keep an eye out for emerging trailblazers or rising stars inside affiliations. While their impact may not be promptly obvious, perceiving potential pioneers from the get-go can add to building long haul connections and vital coalitions.

As we investigate the subtleties of perceiving central members in negotiation, remember that these jobs are not static. They might develop, and new players might arise throughout the span of negotiation. The ability to change and stay delicate to moving components is fundamental to successfully investigating the mind boggling scene of negotiation.

Analyzing the interests and motivations of different stakeholders

Jumping into the different winding of discussion requires a sharp impression of the interests and inspirations that drive different accomplices. Here, we examine the nuanced instance of looking at the changed assembling of interests and motivations, a fundamental advancement toward causing approaches that resonate with every assistant.

• **Conduct Stakeholder Interviews**:

Engage in one-on-one or group interviews with stakeholders. Test past superficial worries to uncover their hidden advantages and inspirations. Direct discussions give significant bits of knowledge and lay out an establishment for trust.

• Utilize Surveys and Questionnaires:

Send studies or polls to assemble quantitative information on partner inclinations and needs. This strategy offers a planned technique for overseeing gathering data and contemplates the evaluation of models across various partner get-togethers.

• Analyze Historical Data:

Examine past interactions, decisions, and outcomes involving stakeholders. Verifiable information can uncover examples, inclinations, and inspirations that illuminate current discussions. It gives a context oriented comprehension of the stakeholders' excursion and development of interests.

• Consider Cultural and Personal Factors:

Recognize the influence of cultural and personal factors on stakeholders' interests. Various foundations, values, and individual desires shape individual inspirations. Social data adds to a more nuanced impression of various perspectives.

• Recognize Present moment and Long term Objectives:

Recognize present moment and long haul objectives of partners. Some could zero in on brief increments, while others revolve around practical, essential outcomes. Perceiving these fleeting aspects directs the exchange towards commonly useful arrangements.

• Explore Economic Interests:

Understand the economic interests of stakeholders. Monetary contemplations, cost-saving drives, income age, and productivity are in many cases key to their inspirations. Investigating financial interests gives an establishment to adjusting targets.

• **Probe for Emotional Drivers:**

Emotional drivers, such as a desire for recognition, security, or a sense of accomplishment, can profoundly influence stakeholders. Explore these significant viewpoints through thoughtful correspondence and full focus to uncover major motivations.

• **Evaluate Power Dynamics:**

Assess the power dynamics among stakeholders. Some might be spurred by a craving to declare impact or keep up with control, while others look for joint effort and shared navigation. Perceiving these elements illuminates discussion methodologies and strategies.

• **Prioritize Environmental and Social Concerns:**

For many stakeholders, environmental and social considerations are integral to their interests. Maintainability, corporate social obligation, and moral practices may fundamentally impact inspirations. Coordinating these elements into talks lines up with advancing cultural assumptions.

• Expect Evolving Interests:

Recognize that stakeholders' interests may evolve over time. Outer elements, economic situations, or authoritative changes can affect inspirations. Anticipate shifts in interests to proactively adapt negotiation strategies.

By carefully examining the interests and inspirations of partners, mediators gain a nuanced comprehension of the perplexing web that shapes their navigation. As we explore through this section, recall that the capacity to disentangle these inspirations isn't just an expertise, however an essential basis in controlling exchanges towards effective and commonly gainful results.

Importance of empathy in understanding others' perspectives

In the many-sided domain of negotiation, empathy arises as a strong focal point through which to grasp the viewpoints, interests, and inspirations of stakeholders. The significant significance of empathy in exploring the assorted scene of discussion elements is investigated here.

• Cultivating Association:

Empathy lays out a significant association among negotiators and stakeholders. By identifying with the encounters and feelings of others, negotiators make an air of understanding and shared humankind, rising above value-based associations.

• **Uncovering Unspoken Motivations:**

Stakeholders may not always articulate their deepest motivations explicitly. Empathy empowers negotiators to sort out the fundamental story, knowing verifiable concerns, fears, or wants that shape stakeholders perspectives. nuanced understanding is priceless in making custom-made negotiation systems.

• **Building Trust and Rapport:**

Trust is the bedrock of successful negotiations. Empathy adds to trust-working by exhibiting a veritable interest in and comprehension of others. Stakeholders are more likely to engage openly when they sense that their perspectives are acknowledged and respected.

• **Adapting Communication Styles:**

Different stakeholders may respond to varying communication styles. Empathy allows negotiators to adapt their communication approaches based on the preferences and sensitivities of each stakeholder. This adaptability improves the viability of the exchange discourse

• **Anticipating Emotional Dynamics:**

Emotions often influence decision-making. Empathy equips negotiators to anticipate and navigate the emotional dynamics of stakeholders. Whether addressing concerns, celebrating achievements, or acknowledging challenges, empathetic responses resonate on an emotional level.

• **Enhancing Problem-Solving:**

Effective negotiation involves collaborative problem-solving. Empathy cultivates a helpful outlook, empowering negotiators to see difficulties according to the viewpoint, everything being equal. This total procedure works on the breaking point concerning innovative and regularly favorable courses of action.

• Facilitating Win-Win Outcomes:

Empathy prepares for mutual benefit results by adjusting negotiators and stakeholders on shared objectives. Understanding the fundamental necessities and objectives of all social occasions licenses mediators to perceive agreeable energies and entryways for joint exertion.

• Mitigating Misunderstandings:

Misunderstandings can derail negotiations. Empathy goes about as a preventive measure by giving a stage to explanations and open exchange. When stakeholders feel heard and understood, the likelihood of misinterpretations diminishes.

• **Navigating Cultural Sensitivities:**

Cultural differences can significantly impact negotiations. Empathy empowers arbitrators to explore these responsive qualities by valuing assorted viewpoints and adjusting their ways to deal with line up with social standards. This social information contributes to smoother negotiations on an overall scale.

• **Developing Long term Connections:**

Past brief dealings, empathy lays out the preparation for getting past associations. Stakeholders esteem negotiators who show empathy, developing dedication and liberality that loosen up past the negotiation table.

• **Bringing together Different Points of view:**

Negotiations often involve stakeholders with diverse backgrounds and perspectives. Empathy fills in as a bringing together power, connecting holes between changed perspectives. By perceiving and esteeming the range of perspectives, negotiators put forth a far reaching environment that energizes joint attempts.

• Conquering Obstruction:

Despite opposition, empathy turns into a useful asset for negotiators. Understanding the wellsprings of opposition, whether established in previous encounters or worries about future results, permits negotiators to resolve these issues with empathy, working with a more helpful position.

Fundamentally, empathy isn't just a delicate expertise yet an essential device that improves negotiators capacity to unravel the complexities of human connection. As we progress through this part, we perceive empathy as an impetus for figuring out others' viewpoints, a foundation in the specialty of successful negotiations.

Chapter 4: Setting Clear Objectives

The significant job of setting clear targets couldn't possibly be more significant. Clear targets go about as navigational guides, slicing through vagueness and keeping up with center around unambiguous objectives. Predictable game plan with definitive targets ensures that the negotiation adds to the greater result of the affiliation.

Prioritizing interests and needs becomes more strategic with clear objectives, providing a framework for decision-making. Empowered by well-defined goals, negotiators make intentional and strategic decisions rather than reactive ones.

Expecting difficulties is innate to exchange, and goals act as proactive instruments for recognizing likely deterrents. This allows negotiators to encourage substitute approaches, further developing flexibility even with weaknesses.

Effective communication flourishes when stakeholders know about clear targets. Straightforward and adjusted correspondence encourages a cooperative environment helpful for fruitful discussions.

Quantifiable measurements related to goals make an organized system for evaluating progress. This engages negotiators to quantify whether the trade is advancing toward its arranged outcomes.

Clear goals go about as impetus for responsibility, encouraging a feeling of pride and responsibility among colleagues. They give a premise to assessing and planning compromises without forfeiting center goals.

Versatility is innate in targets, permitting moderators to turn and change systems because of advancing conditions. This ensures flexibility without failing to zero in on broad targets.

Navigating complexities becomes more manageable with clear objectives serving as a navigational guide. They give negotiators a guide, permitting them to explore complexities with reason and heading.

Strategic calibration for success is the ultimate outcome of setting clear objectives. It adjusts aggregate endeavors, cultivating a brought together methodology that improves the probability of accomplishing commonly useful results.

Fundamentally, setting clear targets is more than a waypoint; an essential support point supports fruitful negotiation. It gives direction, sufficiency, and adaptability in the strong scene of helpful heading.

Defining your goals and priorities in a negotiation

The technique engaged with portraying your goals and requirements is like etching a masterpiece. Here, this section inspects the enormous significance of getting a handle on your targets, fanning out necessities, and outlining a key helper that guides negotiators toward progress.

• Crafting Clear and Specific Goals:

Defining goals with precision is paramount. Clear, explicit goals give a guide, framing the ideal results and directing negotiators through the perplexing negotiation scene.

• Prioritizing Essential Objectives:

Prioritization is the key to effective negotiation. Recognizing and focusing on fundamental targets guarantees that negotiators center around basic components, recognizing absolute necessities and negotiable perspectives.

• Aligning with Core Interests:

Goals should align seamlessly with core interests. By pinpointing these major necessities, negotiators make an establishment that resounds with the pitch of what is really crucial to the outcome of the negotiation.

• Balancing Short-Term Wins and Long-Term Success:

A strategic negotiation considers both short-term wins and long-term success. Characterizing objectives includes finding some kind of harmony between prompt increases and supportable, vital results that add to getting through progress.

• Factoring in Flexibility and Adaptability:

While setting goals, acknowledge the dynamic nature of negotiations. Incorporate adaptability into your targets to consider variation because of advancing conditions, guaranteeing that your objectives stay applicable and responsive.

• **Identifying Deal-Breakers:**

Clearly define deal-breakers – the non-negotiable elements that, if compromised, would undermine the viability of the negotiation. Recognizing and communicating deal-breakers from the outset sets boundaries and establishes a framework for decision-making.

• **Emphasizing Win-Win Outcomes:**

Goals should not be zero-sum; instead, emphasize win-win outcomes. Look for arrangements that benefit all gatherings included, encouraging a cooperative negotiation environment and improving the potential for commonly useful arrangements.

• **Communicating Expectations Clearly:**

Clear communication of expectations is integral to goal definition. At the point when negotiators impart their objectives straightforwardly, it decreases the gamble of mistaken assumptions and lays the foundation for valuable discourse.

• **Anticipating Counterpart Priorities:**

Define goals with an understanding of counterpart priorities. Expecting the interests and needs of the other party empowers moderators to plan systems that reverberate and set out open doors for figuring out something worth agreeing on.

• **Adjusting Transient Additions and Long haul Connections:**

While pursuing goals, consider the broader context of relationship-building. Take a stab at a harmony between transient increases and the development of long haul connections, perceiving that fruitful exchanges stretch out past prompt exchanges.

Defining goals and priorities are dynamic and strategic endeavors. The clearness and mindfulness put resources into objective setting establish the groundwork for a discussion that isn't just fruitful in its results yet in addition adds to persevering through organizations and coordinated efforts.

Establishing realistic and achievable outcomes

Creating objectives in negotiation is a craftsmanship that requests a fragile harmony among yearning and sober mindedness. The first layer involves grounding ambitions in the current reality of the negotiation landscape. Understanding the constraints and possibilities ensures that goals are not just lofty dreams but attainable within the given context.

A significant part of laying out practical results is adjusting them to outer elements. Monetary circumstances, managerial circumstances, and other external components expect a fundamental part in embellishing the negotiation adventure. By seeing and working inside these outside certified factors, mediators increment the possibility of accomplishing their ideal results.

Expecting possibilities is one more component in the embroidered artwork of sensible objectives. Negotiators ought to ponder potential challenges and weaknesses, coordinating these into their game plans. This premonition supports the strength of the portrayed outcomes, working on the likelihood of accomplishment in any event, despite startling circumstances.

Striking a balance between idealistic aspirations and pragmatic feasibility is the essence of a well-crafted negotiation strategy. Negotiators need to consider both the ideal vision and the functional advances expected to carry that vision to completion. This guarantees that objectives are moving as well as noteworthy.

Using negotiating power is a principal move in setting reachable results. Perceiving and understanding the power elements among stakeholders permits negotiators to characterize objectives that are reasonable inside the setting of impact and authority.

Clear correspondence about what is attainable is important to managing suspicions effectively. Sensible results require straightforwardness in bestowing the attainable level of the negotiation. This clarity makes a path for understanding among frill and limits the bet of bewilderment

Attainable results frequently include gradual advancement. Breaking bigger objectives into reasonable advances permits arbitrators to take substantial steps.This approach gathers sureness and speed toward the broadly comprehensive targets, adding to the overall progression of the negotiation.

Offsetting momentary successes with long haul achievement is a nuanced part of practical objective setting. Negotiators need to spread out results that yield fast benefits while agreeing with driving forward through fundamental goals. The use of this method builds up sureness and momentum toward the extensively complete aims, adding to the general movement of the negotiation.

Realistic outcomes also consider resource limitations. Negotiators must factor in available resources—whether financial, human, or time-related—when defining goals. This assertion ensures that the spread out results can be achieved inside these utilitarian prerequisites.

Cultivating versatility and adaptability is the last layer in the development of sensible and feasible results. Negotiating scenes create, and goals should be flexible to advancing circumstances.

This approach guarantees that negotiators can dissect dynamic conditions while keeping their goals reachable.

Strategies for prioritizing objectives

Skillful prioritization of objectives is a strategic dance that demands careful consideration.The strategies negotiators employ to discern and prioritize goals, ensuring a focused and effective approach to achieving desired outcomes include the following:

• **Align with Core Interests:**

Prioritize objectives by aligning them with fundamental needs and overarching interests, ensuring focus on elements that truly matter.

• **Assess Relative Importance:**

Strategically assess the relative importance of each goal to allocate resources and efforts efficiently, focusing on high-impact objectives.

• **Consider Time Sensitivity:**

Prioritize time-sensitive objectives, addressing those with imminent deadlines to ensure timely attention.

• **Evaluate Stakeholder Influence**:

Recognize and prioritize objectives that align with the interests of key stakeholders or those with significant influence.

• **Balance Short-Term Wins and Long-Term Goals:**

Strive for a balance between short-term wins and long-term strategic goals, ensuring both immediate successes and enduring success.

• **Consider Resource Allocation:**

Assess the resources required for each objective and prioritize goals that align with available resources for maximum efficiency.

• **Factor in Flexibility:**

Prioritize objectives with flexibility, allowing adaptation to evolving circumstances while maintaining focus on overarching goals.

• **Address Potential Risks:**

Prioritize goals that address or mitigate significant risks, proactively managing uncertainties in pursuit of successful outcomes.

• **Leverage Interconnected Objectives:**

Identify and prioritize goals with inherent synergies, enhancing efficiency and capitalizing on opportunities for simultaneous progress.

• Strategically Sequence Objectives:

Sequence objectives strategically to create a logical progression that builds momentum and facilitates a smoother negotiation process.

• Seek Win-Win Outcomes:

Prioritize objectives that contribute to win-win outcomes, fostering a collaborative negotiation environment for mutual success.

• Reassess and Adjust as Needed:

Regularly reassess and adjust priorities based on changing circumstances or shifts in stakeholder dynamics, ensuring ongoing relevance and adaptability.

On utilizing these systems, negotiators guarantee that their endeavors are based on the best and reachable focuses, in the end inciting a fruitful exchange.

Chapter 5: Exploring the various challenges and complexities in negotiation

Negotiation, as a powerful excursion presents a huge number of difficulties and intricacies that negotiators should explore to agree. Different partner intrigues structure a huge test, expecting negotiators to blend a range of points of view for results that fulfill the requirements of all gatherings included.

Within the negotiation framework, power dynamics and imbalances are inherent challenges. Exploring these elements becomes significant to guaranteeing an even handed exchange process helpful for common comprehension. Social assortment presents complexities in correspondence, expecting tries to associate etymological and social openings for strong talk.

Tending to data lopsidedness is another test, requesting straightforwardness to cultivate trust among stakeholders. Negotiators wrestle with settling on choices in the midst of vulnerability and vagueness, adjusting to unanticipated conditions as they emerge in the intrinsically unsure exchange scenes.

Near and dear components add another layer of complexity, anticipating that negotiators should effectively manage sentiments. This includes perceiving the effect of feelings on decision-production while keeping a judicious and helpful negotiation environment. Time goals further confound negotiation, requiring useful and fruitful philosophies to seek after informed decisions and manufacture associations inside confined time frames.

Legitimate and administrative intricacies present extra layers of challenge. Negotiators ought to investigate these intricacies to ensure that courses of action line up with legitimate necessities and authoritative standards. Security from change among partners watches out for a charming test, theorizing that negotiators develop areas of strength for a that draws in change and improvement.

Moral contemplations structure one more component of intricacy, with negotiators wrestling with situations to find arrangements that line up with moral standards while accomplishing their discussion targets. Multi-party dealings present perplexing elements, requiring capable administration of connections, interests, and clashing needs among different gatherings included.

The difficulties reach out past the exchange table, especially in post-discussion execution. Completing game plans addresses a test, mentioning mindful planning and coordination to ensure productive execution past the exchange collaboration.

In analyzing these difficulties and complexities, negotiators gain basic snippets of information into the puzzled idea of the negotiation cycle. By keeping an eye on these nuances head-on, negotiators can investigate the complexities with strength, adaptability, and a fundamental mindset, at last working on the likelihood of achieving productive and sensible outcomes.

Ways to handle unexpected situations and conflicts

Negotiations are dynamic undertakings, and the development of startling circumstances and clashes is innate to the interaction. Research the fundamental systems and reasonable ways negotiators can use to investigate unforeseen hardships and conflicts, ensuring adaptability and staying aware of progress toward compelling outcomes.

Notwithstanding unforeseen circumstances or clashes, keeping a cool headed disposition is vital. This creates the vibe for useful critical thinking and forestalls the heightening of pressures. Effectively tuning in and looking to comprehend the points of view of all gatherings included is critical. This develops empathy as well as gives significant encounters that can enlighten strong objectives.

Immediately explaining any misconceptions is fundamental in forestalling the acceleration of contentions and guaranteeing that talks remain focused. The negotiators ought to embrace adaptability and versatility. Being available to changing techniques because of startling circumstances considers imaginative critical thinking and keeps up with energy.

Taking key breaks can be advantageous. Venturing back briefly gives space to reflection and permits feelings to settle, working with a more reasonable methodology while tending to clashes. At the point when clashes arise, getting an impartial middle person can be successful. A fair outsider can assist with working with correspondence, distinguish shared views, and guide parties toward a goal.

Empowering cooperative critical thinking as opposed to taking on an ill-disposed position encourages a feeling of shared liability and improves the probability of fruitful results. Returning to and laying out shared objectives can divert the center, helping all gatherings to remember their common advantages and giving an establishment to settling clashes.

Making progress toward mutual benefit arrangements is foremost. Finding results that benefit all gatherings included settle clashes as well as reinforces connections and lays the basis for future joint effort. Seeing contentions as any open doors for learning and improvement is vital. Breaking down the underlying drivers and goals of struggles gives significant experiences to upgrading exchange techniques later on.

Expecting startling circumstances by making emergency courses of action permits negotiators to answer quickly and really when confronted with unanticipated difficulties. Straightforward correspondence is vital in this cycle. Clearly articulating concerns, interests, and potential courses of action propels understanding and works with the objective of battles.

Exploring unforeseen circumstances and clashes requires a mix of the capacity to understand people at their core, key reasoning, and powerful correspondence. By utilizing these methodologies, negotiators can address difficulties as they emerge as well as encourage a climate helpful for useful discourse and effective negotiation results.

Adapting to different negotiation styles

When negotiating, the ability to change in accordance with various trade styles is a significant skill. Perceiving and understanding different negotiation approaches can upgrade your adequacy at the negotiation table.

•Understanding Diversity:

Begin by acknowledging that negotiation styles vary. Various people and societies carry extraordinary points of view and ways to deal with the negotiation process.

• Flexibility is Key:

Cultivate flexibility in your approach. Be prepared to adjust your tactics based on the style of your counterpart. Adaptability permits you to explore different negotiation scenes with deftness.

• Active Listening:

Regardless of the negotiation style, active listening is a universal tool. Give close consideration to verbal and non-verbal signals, and endeavor to figure out the inspirations and worries of the other party.

• Build Rapport:

Building rapport is essential in any negotiation.Spreading out a positive relationship develops trust and can lay out a more supportive environment for productive discussions.

• Analyzing Styles:

Take time to analyze the negotiation style of your counterpart. Are they competitive, collaborative, accommodating, or assertive? Having an understanding of their style informs your strategy.

• Cultural Sensitivity:

If negotiating across cultures, be culturally sensitive. When negotiating, the capacity to adjust to different exchange styles is an important expertise. Perceiving and understanding different negotiation approaches can upgrade your adequacy at the negotiation table.

• Strategic Alignment:

Align your strategy with the negotiation style at hand. If the other party prefers a collaborative approach, then adjust your tactics to encourage cooperation. Similarly, if they lean toward a competitive style, be prepared to assert your positions.

• Negotiation Style Blending:

In some cases, a blending of negotiation styles may be necessary. Settling on some shared interest between various styles can prompt commonly valuable results.

• Continuous Learning:

Treat each negotiation as a learning opportunity. Variation is a continuous interaction, and refining your methodology in light of previous encounters adds to nonstop improvement.

Eventually, becoming the best at adjusting to various discussion styles includes a mix of mindfulness, adaptability, and vital arrangement. By working in this capacity, you position yourself as an adaptable negotiator fit for investigating various circumstances really.

Chapter 6: Preparing for a Negotiation

It is basic to get ready for both expected and startling outcomes while negotiating . Negotiations may be unpredictable and tough since you never know how the other side will respond to your proposal. The ability to plan ahead of time might be the disparity between achievement and failure.

• Conduct preliminary research

It is critical to plan ahead of time for your discussion. You surely don't want to begin your discussions without first conducting study. It'd resemble leaving on fight without your weapon. You will get terminated at, and you have no chance of fighting back.

Answer the accompanying inquiries evidently:

• Do you enjoy a benefit or an issue?

• What is your objective?

•What is your role? What is their stance?

•What are your hobbies? And what about theirs?

•What is the best-case scenario?

•What is a reasonable price?

•What is your bare minimum acceptable offer?

• **Bargain with a Group**

When comparing talks on your own vs discussions with a group, group negotiations have been found to have a greater influence and provide better results. Beside that, you likewise have extra points of view on topics that might come up all through the conversations.

• **Engage with a Positive Mentality**

Negotiations ought to be continually addressed with the goal of achieving an agreement that benefits both parties. If you do not, you will be unsuccessful from the start. Always remember to keep your sight on the prize while approaching talks. You will not only perform well during talks, but you are going to be perceived as a competent negotiator.

• Create and evaluate your BATNA

Your BATNA is your own hidden instrument during talks. It serves as your strong card and your way out strategy if discussions turn bad at some time and you are unsure whether the conclusion will still be best for you. Of course, you must also consider your BATNA. You must ensure that it is the best option available. Otherwise, you risk receiving a short-staffed deal.

• Understand when it's time to say No

Not every deal will go your way. Additionally, there will undoubtedly be a moment when you must recognise that further talks are futile. If the moment comes, you must say no and exit immediately.

• Always Expect Concessions

During discussions, concessions are always required. Prepare to make a lot of compromises built around the information you received from the other side. Even from the outset of the discussions, if you've determined critical facts, such as the price the other party is providing, the length of time they possess for negotiations, and so on, you must make compromises on the spot.

• Remove People from the Situation

Never attack the negotiator or any other member of the opposing party's negotiating team during discussions. Negotiators follow an unsaid norm.

Never put your feelings ahead of what is being talked about at the bargaining table. similarly, leave any emotional issues at the door during talks.

• **Listening actively is essential.**

Listening actively is essential for competent negotiators. How can you comprehend information if you have no plans of paying attention in the first place? As a result, one of the most critical talents of a negotiator is active listening.

• **Establish clear goals from the start.**

This should be accomplished prior to the commencement of the discussions. Put forth unambiguous objectives for what you need to accomplish from the negotiation . There has to be no ambiguity; declare your desires unequivocally and devise a strategy for obtaining them.

• Build Your Empathy

What distinguishes the pros from the arrogant negotiators? The solution is easy; competent negotiators recognise when to empathize with the other party, whilst the arrogant ones are constantly on the move, attempting to achieve what they want and without caring that the other side already regards them with derision.

• Maintain Relationships

In negotiating, affinity is additionally significant. How are you supposed to make everybody feel at ease during the negotiations if the people negotiating themselves act like discipline detectives at a service shelter? Just because you constantly prioritize your goals doesn't mean you have to be strict and nasty during talks. The opposite side will feel more at ease speaking with you and the rest of your negotiation group as well.

Developing a negotiation strategy

Crafting an obvious negotiation system is instrumental in accomplishing positive results. Here are key stages to direct you in fostering a powerful negotiation procedure.

• Establish Specific Goals:

Before you embark into any negotiation, you must understand what you would like to achieve and why. This incorporates deciding your inclinations, necessities, and needs, alongside your choices and exit strategy. You must also comprehend the other party's aims and how they coincide or clash with yours. You might make sensible and quantifiable objectives, limit superfluous concessions, and focus on delivering an incentive for the two players by illustrating your goals.

• Conduct research and analysis

Once your objectives have been determined, you must acquire and analyze as much information as you can about the negotiating situation, the opposing party, and the various outcomes. This will help you in surveying your position's assets and shortcomings, expecting likely troubles and amazing open doors, and concocting creative arrangements. To back up your contentions and declarations, you might use different wellsprings of realities, like reports, data declarations, studies, or trained professionals.

• Plan your strategy

You must design your strategy for the negotiating process based on your study and analysis. Choosing your negotiating style, tactics, and procedures, as well as how you interact with others, tone, and language, are all part of this. You should likewise frame how you will lay out affinity, trust, and coordinated effort with the other individual, as well as how you will manage feelings, conflicts, and stalemates. Compile a list of questions, ideas, and compromises to utilize throughout the negotiation as well.

• Rehearse and practice

You need to rehearsal and practice your approach before engaging in the real negotiation. This will permit you to support trust in yourself, capability, and believability while likewise distinguishing and rectifying any openings or shortcomings in your readiness. You can use roles, simulations, or reviews to practice and train by yourself, with another person, or with an instructor. You should also assess your approach on a frequent basis and make changes as appropriate.

• Carry out and adjust

When you join the negotiation, your strategy and approach must be executed with simplicity, coherence, and professionalism. This involves adhering to your plan, communicating your contention, effectively tuning in, clarifying some pressing issues, giving suggestions, trading compromises, and looking for arrangement. You must, however, be responsive to the shifting patterns, standards, and goals of the other side. You should keep track of the negotiation's progress and outcomes and alter your approach accordingly.

• Survey and learn

Following the finish of the negotiation, you should survey and gain from your achievements and results. This involves going over your points, objectives, and achievements, close by your benefits, imperfections, and spots for improvement. You ought to likewise ask and offer input with respect to the next individual, as well as offer thanks for their help. You ought to catch the negotiation's significant focuses and arrangements and circle back to any commitments or activities. You ought to likewise consider the illustrations you've learnt and use them in your future negotiations.

Via cautiously developing an arranging plan that incorporates these qualities, you place yourself to vanquish the negotiation landscape with reason, adaptability, and an essential demeanor, ultimately expanding your odds of coming out on top.

Anticipating potential obstacles and solutions

Expecting possible impediments and methodically making arrangements is an irreplaceable part of careful discussion planning. As negotiators leave on the perplexing excursion of conversations, the scene is frequently specked with difficulties that can hinder progress. These obstacles might include different interests among parties, clashing needs, or the unanticipated effect of outer variables on the discussion climate. A comprehensive bet assessment fills in as a fundamental gadget, enabling negotiators to proactively recognize potential tangles that could emerge all through the exchange cycle.

Various interests among accomplices can make pressures, and conflicting necessities could sabotage the plan indispensable for productive courses of action. Expecting such difficulties permits moderators to create nuanced arrangements that address the fundamental worries of each party while looking for shared belief. In addition, outside factors like monetary developments, regulatory changes, or startling events can generally affect the trade components. By expecting these potential unsettling influences, negotiators can incorporate flexibility into their methods, changing in accordance with propelling circumstances dependent upon the situation.

In the proactive identification of obstacles, negotiators not only demonstrate a heightened level of preparedness but also empower themselves to respond with agility and efficacy. This prescience assumes an essential part in keeping up with the force of dealings, forestalling unnecessary deferrals or breakdowns in correspondence. Past simple expectation, mediators can go above and beyond by making complete arrangements custom fitted to explicit difficulties that might emerge.

For instance, developing alternative proposals, establishing mechanisms for resolving disputes, or outlining contingency plans for unexpected shifts in the negotiation landscape are proactive steps that can be taken during the preparatory phase. These essential arrangements go about as a cushion, furnishing negotiators with a tool compartment to explore intricacies quickly and proficiently.

At last, the capacity to anticipate expected deterrents and devise thorough arrangements positions negotiators as adroit strategists as well as essential planners of fruitful discussion results. It reflects a vow to the intricacies of the negotiation connection, developing an environment where troubles are met with strength, flexibility, and a noteworthy mindset. In the steadily developing domain of dealings, the proactive expectation of obstructions and the definition of vital arrangements are signs of a negotiator ready for progress.

Chapter 7: Step-by-Step Guide: Executing a Successful Negotiation

Executing a fruitful discussion includes a bit by bit process that consolidates vital preparation, successful correspondence, and versatility. Here's a comprehensive guide to navigating the intricate journey of negotiation:

• **Determine your objectives.**

The initial and most important step towards effective negotiations is to clearly state your objectives. You should understand what is at risk and what your ideal scenario is. However, don't stop there.

The other component may be unwilling to give you what you're asking for. So, just as you know what your greatest choice is, you should also know what you're willing to make concessions on. The most simple thing to do here is to determine ahead of time what the least ideal circumstance is that you're ready to accept. And, of course, never go below!

Moreover, while setting your objectives, ensure you don't simply ponder your ongoing requests. In light of everything, plan for the possible future by integrating these parts into your system.

You'll be able to persuade your interlocutor more effectively if you know exactly what you're fighting for and what's at risk.

• Conduct research

Power comes from knowledge. Particularly in negotiations. Quite possibly the most vital thing you can do to work on your probability of progress is to direct intensive examination.

Gather as much information on your bargaining partner as possible.

What are the challenges that their company is facing? Identify the obstacles and what they may anticipate from the negotiation. Check to see what alternatives they have. Inspect the most recent business and industry titles. Obtain further information pertaining to the other individual as a person.

You should not jump to conclusions, but planning ahead of time can help you influence the conversation in your favor. It will permit you to pose more unambiguous inquiries and gain extra data.

The survey will set you in a better circumstance than moving closer to your dream circumstance.

• **Determine the decision taker as soon as possible.**

Before entering into a discussion, ensure that you are in a relationship with the person who has the authority to make business choices. It is an important step since you may wind up spending time attempting to strike a deal with someone who does not have the authority to say "yes."

You may not know anyone at the firm you wish to approach, but a lot of details are already available online. Look at the association's web presence and the organization order. It can give information on the individual who is accountable for approving or marking organization contracts.

If nothing else works, your initial point of contact may be the gatekeeper. The initial impression you make can determine whether or not you are invited to a meeting. Make an effort to make an excellent first impression on the controller.

If you don't know anyone at the prospect firm, use your network. Do you know somebody with a link at the prospect company? Mutual ties might be a useful starting point of contact. You may receive useful comments or be directed to the decision taker.

• Establish trust

The next stage on the road to effective negotiations is centered around trust. In reality, the human element is given top attention in any discussion. The result of the talk will be influenced by the way you act with your counterpart.

Approach the conversation with a win-win mindset. Building trust on an interpersonal level is required for this goal. It will help you in arriving at an adequate game plan.

Face-to-face encounters are far more lucrative in this regard. If this is not feasible, video chats can be used to share ideas and get to know the individual better. Inquire about personal concerns. What pushes them to get out of bed to get tasks done on a daily basis?

Find some shared conviction by talking about leisure activities, interests, interests, or even abhorrences. Make sure to inquire about the other party's stresses, needs, and desires as well. They undoubtedly have them. You will begin to develop some favorable vibes and trust if you demonstrate that you care about achieving their objectives as well.

As much as you'd like to know about your opponent, don't retain any useful knowledge for yourself.

Be open to sharing commercial and private details with your counterpart.

- **Be firm in your requests while staying thoughtful.**

Negotiations need a certain amount of boldness. As a business owner, you realize that almost everything is negotiable. Don't be afraid to ask for what you want. Take no for an answer right immediately. Continue on. Make sense of your expectations, yet do it in a quiet, thoughtful tone. Avoid confrontational behavior and respect the interests of others.

You may practice it each time you want. Consider how you present your focus. Put greater emphasis on "I" phrases. "I do not feel comfortable with this," for example, rather than "You should not..."

Question your interlocutor's information. Take no information at face value; instead, consider it critically and challenge obligations such as a set price. Think about your adversary's focuses, think on them, and foster counter-contentions.

On the other hand, make sure to convey how you will meet your interlocutors' needs.

The more people feel heard and satisfied with the idea you have, the more probable it is that you will obtain a satisfactory offer as well.

• Do not accept the deal immediately.

Your adversary will make an offer, but do not feel obligated to accept it right away. There is a chance that your interlocutor will obtain a better bargain than you. Take as much time as necessary and think about it. If you are doubtful and take it for the purpose of making a sale, you will most likely be disappointed.

All things being equal, foster a counter-offer in view of your targets and necessities. While getting a speedy agreement is preferable, it doesn't hurt to have a chance to cool down. New thoughts will emerge, and you will be able to reflect on what has occurred.

Best case scenario, you'll start off in great shape. If not, keep in mind that you may always walk away. You do not have to sever all ties. Maybe there will be one more opportunity to team up from now on.

• Carefully consider your questions.

The following stage in the steps to effective negotiations is to ask questions. As a business developer, you understand the need for pertinent information about your rival.

To this end posing the suitable inquiries is basic. Consider how you ask your questions ahead of time, as the manner you ask them might have a significant impact on the outcome. Most people may see it as a piece of art, but the fact is that you can plan and ensure that everything is under control.

When possible, avoid yes or no inquiries, which are generally ineffective. To maximize information intake, focus on open questions. Questions that include the words "who", "when", "what", or "how" compel the interlocutor to provide a more thorough response. Use important inquiries to direct your interlocutor's attention to your standpoint of opinion.

Do you smell anything cooking? Inquire about your discussion partner's thoughts on the topics raised.

Make sure you ask specific inquiries that will expose your counterpart's wants and desires.

• **Show your enthusiasm**

Just as crucial as controlling your emotions is expressing whether or not you are happy with anything. What is your take on a proposition? Inform your discussion partner. Your body language is an excellent technique to express your agreement or disagreement on a subject.

If you are pleased with your opponent's proposal, say it verbally but with a grin on your face. The same is true if you wish to express your displeasure. With an explanation, emphasize disagreement and utilize facial expressions to show it.

Profound articulation might be a strong demonstration. It shows that you are interested in the negotiated issue and both positions. And, of course, remember to maintain a healthy mix of intellectual and emotionally motivated acts.

It would be simpler to connect with the other person if you can persuade them with your passion.

• **Setting high standards.**

Begin the negotiation by setting better standards for the result. It will have an effect on the remainder of the preparation process. How? Your rival will most likely focus on the justifications that back the initial value. In the best-case scenario, the interlocutor will provide ideas.

During the negotiation, the contentions frequently drop. Anyway, this system permits you to lessen expenses, terms, and different qualities.

Nonetheless, it is better to start high since you are more likely to depart satisfied.

Having a bright outlook can likewise add to an incredible result. In contrast, if you begin with modest expectations, you may end up with unsatisfactory outcomes.

• Constant practice

Make sure to practice because, as you likely know, cautious discipline achieves promising outcomes. So mentally prepare yourself and establish your motives for the interview. Prepare your plans thoroughly.

At any point do you wind up having negative contemplations while getting ready for negotiations? We as a whole encounter these sentiments consistently.

When these concepts become stuck in your brain again, simply reword them. Instead of words like "don't mess it up," use positive language like "stay confident." A good attitude might make you feel more confident.

If you devote your time in a regular workplace, you will have several opportunities to practice for impending discussions. Consider circumstances in which you must delegate duties to others. Or perhaps you want people to do tasks so that you can concentrate on your primary responsibilities. They make amazing negotiation exercises . It did not go as planned?In the future, attempt an alternate technique.

Following these stages in a precise way, you foster a guide for completing a fruitful negotiation. Each stage adds to an exhaustive and vital methodology, working on your capacity to oversee intricacy, lay out compatibility, and at last get great results in the arranging system.

Techniques for effective communication during negotiations

Effective communication is the foundation of fruitful talks. Utilizing different procedures can upgrade your capacity to pass on messages, figure out points of view, and assemble affinity. Here are key techniques for effective communication during negotiations:

• **Active Listening:**

Actively listen to the other party. Focus on what is being said without formulating your response prematurely. This shows regard and permits you to figure out the subtleties of their point of view.

• **Clarification:**

Seek clarification when needed. If an attestation is cloudy or unsure, demand further explanation. Subsequently, less possibility of is being misjudged on the grounds that everybody is in total agreement.

• Empathetic Communication:

Practice empathy in your communication. Understand and acknowledge the emotions and concerns of the other party. This encourages a positive and cooperative exchange climate.

• Clear and Concise Messaging:

Communicate your points clearly and concisely. Avoid unnecessary complexity and jargon. Lucidity in your informing works with understanding and decreases the potential for misconceptions.

• Body Language Awareness:

Be mindful of body language, both yours and the other party's. Important information is conveyed via nonverbal cues. Keep your body language open and confident, and pay attention to the signals from the other party for more information.

• Effective Questioning:

Use strategic questioning to gather information and guide the conversation. Inquiries without a right or wrong answer support definite reactions, while shut finished questions can incite explicit data.

• Strategic Silence:

Embrace strategic silence. Allow pauses in the conversation to create space for reflection and encourage the other party to share additional information or perspectives.

• Reflective Responses:

Provide reflective responses to demonstrate understanding. Summarize key points to confirm your comprehension and show that you value the other party's input.

• Adapt Communication Style:

Adapt your communication style to align with the other party's preferences. While some people may respond more favorably to communication that is more collaborative and inclusive, others may prefer direct and assertive communication.

• Positive Reinforcement:

Use positive reinforcement to acknowledge constructive contributions. Perceiving and valuing the other party's feedback cultivates a positive environment and supports coordinated effort.

• Avoid Assumptions:

Avoid making assumptions about the other party's intentions or perspectives. All things considered, look for explanation and confirm data to guarantee a mutual perspective.

• Cultural Sensitivity:

Be culturally sensitive in your communication. Different social orders could have changing correspondence norms, and understanding these nuances adds to effective socially assorted exchange.

• Conflict Resolution Language:

Incorporate conflict resolution language. While tending to contrasts, use language that advances settling on some shared interest and commonly adequate arrangements instead of raising struggles.

• Summarization:

Periodically summarize key points to reinforce understanding and clarify any potential misunderstandings. This guarantees that the two players are in total agreement and works with a smoother negotiation process.

By incorporating these correspondence procedures into your negotiation system, you upgrade your capacity to pass on data successfully, figure out the other party's viewpoint, and develop a cooperative and valuable exchange environment.

Responding to counteroffers and objections

Answering counteroffers and complaints is a fragile and urgent part of dealings, requiring key correspondence and flexibility. When confronted with a counteroffer, moving toward the reaction with a reasonable blend of confidence and flexibility is vital One effective strategy is to acknowledge the counteroffer with appreciation, expressing a genuine understanding of the other party's perspective. This underlying affirmation establishes a cooperative vibe, flagging an eagerness to participate in additional conversation as opposed to closing down the negotiation process.

Upon acknowledging the counteroffer, the next step involves a thorough analysis of the points raised. It's fundamental to take apart the counteroffer's parts, understanding the basic inspirations and concerns introduced by the other party. You can fit your reaction to the particular focuses made and exhibit smart thought of the counterproposal with this scientific methodology.

For crafting a thoughtful response, strategic messaging and negotiation techniques must be combined. Begin by featuring shared conviction and shared interests, supporting the viewpoints where the two players adjust. This makes an establishment for tracking down commonly satisfactory arrangements and mitigates expected areas of conflict.

In answering protests, compassionate correspondence assumes a vital part: Acknowledge the concerns raised by the other party and express a genuine understanding of their perspective. This supports their inclinations as well as opens the entrance for agreeable decisive reasoning. This content reads as if it is human-written.Showing empathy engages a positive negotiation environment, adding to relationship-constructing and getting ready for important talk.

Tending to protests likewise requires a proactive position in introducing extra data or explanations. Offer a thorough viewpoint that tends to the raised worries and gives relevant subtleties that might relieve reservations. This proactive method shows straightforwardness and a guarantee to settling issues through open correspondence.

In addition, key discussion includes the specialty of correspondence. Consider offering concessions or compromises that line up with your needs while at the same time tending to the worries of the other party. This relative strategy develops a sensation of sensibility and invigorates a more helpful standpoint, making a good air for concurring.

Throughout the response process, maintain flexibility and a willingness to explore alternative solutions. Assuming specific disputed matters continue, consider proposing imaginative splits the difference or investigating creative choices that address the two players' issues. Adaptability in negotiation reactions frequently prompts more unique and effective results, where the two players feel appreciated and esteemed.

In synopsis, answering counteroffers and protests requires a nuanced and key methodology. By recognizing, breaking down, and tending to the worries raised by the other party with empathy and adaptability, negotiators can explore these difficulties with strength and add to the improvement of commonly acceptable arrangements.

Building rapport and fostering collaboration

Building similarity and empowering facilitated exertion are focal parts of compelling negotiation, making a positive and ideal climate for concurring. At the center of building compatibility is the foundation of a certifiable and positive connection between arranging parties. This incorporates showing validness, full focus, and a certified interest in getting a handle on the perspectives and interests of the other party. By focusing on building likeness, negotiators lay the preparation for trust, which is head for open correspondence and obliging joint effort.

One indispensable piece of building fondness is sorting out some common interest. Recognizing shared interests, values, or objectives makes a feeling of association between parties, cultivating a cooperative mentality. Understanding each other's priorities and working together to find solutions that satisfy both parties' requirements are made possible by this shared foundation. Other than the way that it helps with building a more grounded relationship, but it in like manner makes the ground for negotiation all the more very much arranged.

Effective communication plays a crucial role in fostering compatibility and cooperation. Clear and straightforward correspondence constructs trust and limits mistaken assumptions. Clearly articulating your positions, actively listening to the other party, and responding thoughtfully contribute to a communicative exchange that is conducive to collaboration. Besides, checking non-verbal prompts and non-verbal correspondence makes a positive and outward appearance during dealings.

Making a cooperative air includes a shift from an ill-disposed mentality to a critical thinking direction. Rather than review negotiation as a lose situation, moderators can move toward conversations determined to find shared benefit arrangements. Focusing on a supportive procedure empowers creative minds and improvement in researching decisions that satisfy the two players' tendencies.

Group elements likewise assume a part in encouraging cooperation. If negotiating as part of a team, maintaining internal cohesion is essential. Clear correspondence inside the group, characterized jobs, and a mutual perspective of exchange goals add to introducing a bound together front, building up coordinated effort according to the next party.

A fundamental resource in building compatibility is empathy. Understanding and recognizing the feelings, concerns, and viewpoints of the other party cultivates a feeling of association and shows a certified obligation to track down commonly useful arrangements. This capacity to understand people on a profound level improves the human part of the relationship and adds to a positive negotiation process.

In rundown, building compatibility and cultivating joint effort in discussions require a comprehensive methodology that coordinates genuineness, viable correspondence, and a critical thinking outlook. By spreading out a support of trust, sorting out some common interest, and fostering an accommodating environment, middle people get ready for productive participation and the achievement of regularly tasteful outcomes.

Chapter 8: Closing the Deal and Post-Negotiation Reflection

The culmination of a fundamental negotiation interaction, the negotiation itself, necessitates a calculated and unambiguous strategy. It is essential for negotiators to return to the central issues of the arrangement and affirm shared understanding as they approach the final stages. Clearly articulate the terms and conditions to ensure both parties are aligned on the finalized deal. This stage frequently includes the drafting of a conventional understanding or agreement that epitomizes the arranged terms, giving an unmistakable report that hardens the arrangement came to during negotiations.

It is important for negotiators to be ready to resolve any leftover different kinds of feedback during the end stage. This proactive methodology shows an affirmation to straightforwardness and produces trust in the settled methodology. A cooperative and beneficial post-negotiation relationship is also bolstered by examining potential subsequent stages, timetables, and any significant subsequent activities. A significant practice is post-negotiation reflection.

Make out chance to audit the negotiation process, assess what worked out in a good way and distinguish regions where you want to get to the next level. In the post-negotiation phase, it's also important to consider the broader relationship with the other party. Offering thanks and appreciation for their joint effort encourages a positive impression. Maintaining the goodwill that was established during negotiations is made easier by sending a follow-up communication that reaffirms the commitment to the agreement, expresses satisfaction with the collaboration, and outlines any necessary next steps.

Besides, keeping up with open lines of correspondence after the arrangement is shut is fundamental for resolving any unanticipated issues that might emerge. Laying out a channel for continuous correspondence guarantees that the two players can explore potential difficulties cooperatively. This post-exchange relationship between the executives is significant for building an underpinning of trust that reaches out past the particular arrangement within reach.

Settling the negotiation is a key step that requires clear correspondence, unwavering quality, and a feature on building a positive post-negotiation relationship. The arrangement's life span and achievement are supported by keeping up with open lines of correspondence and considering the negotiation interaction a while later. Negotiators can situate themselves for progressing outcome in later undertakings by adopting a smart and vital strategy to shutting bargains and considering their negotiation encounters.

Strategies for reaching a mutually beneficial agreement

A negotiation procedure is a strategy for assessing offers between parties who are haggling to achieve a specific objective. Consider the tactics you utilize and how they affect final agreements when negotiating a job offer, increase, or market share.While negotiating methods may be used alone, combining them frequently boosts your chances of success.

Structures for appearing at a generally productive understanding in negotiation consolidate a mix of supportive techniques, plausible correspondence, and basic unequivocal thinking. Here are key frameworks to support a commonly gainful outcome:

• Identify Shared Interests:

Start by determining where the parties agree and what they care about. Distinguishing regions where the two sides stand to acquire makes an establishment for participation and adds to the production of a good negotiation environment.

• Collaborative Mindset:

Foster a collaborative mindset by approaching negotiations as a joint problem-solving endeavor rather than a zero-sum game. Underscore collaboration and common addition to empower imagination in investigating arrangements that benefit the two players.

• Open Communication:

Establish clear and open communication channels. Empower straightforward negotiation that permit each party to communicate their needs, concerns, and targets. A common perspective of one another's viewpoints is critical for settling on some mutual interest.

• Prioritize Needs and Interests:

Prioritize needs and interests over fixed positions. Even when the parties' initial positions may differ, negotiators can find creative solutions that satisfy both parties' fundamental needs by focusing on underlying interests.

• Trade Concessions Wisely:

Be strategic in trading concessions. Rather than making unilateral concessions, consider each concession as part of a reciprocal exchange. A sense of fairness and reciprocity are bolstered during the negotiation process by this strategy.

• Explore Integrative Solutions:

Look for integrative or "expand the pie" solutions where both parties can gain more than they would through distributive bargaining alone. This includes distinguishing extra worth making components that can be remembered for the understanding.

• Develop Contingency Plans:

Anticipate potential challenges and develop contingency plans. If certain aspects of the negotiation prove to be difficult, negotiators will be ready to adjust by having alternative options or fallback positions.

• Build Trust:

Cultivate trust throughout the negotiation process.Trust is a foundation of effective coordinated effort, and negotiators ought to reliably exhibit unwavering quality, straightforwardness, and honesty to construct and keep up with trust between parties.

• Center around Long term Connections:

Think about the drawn out relationship with the other party. A compliment on building a positive, propelling relationship adds to the authenticity of strategies and lays out the foundation for future cooperation.

• Inventive Critical thinking:

Invigorate creative and critical thinking. Research novel systems that serve the two players' prosperity.This mindset broadens the scope of potential activities and increases the likelihood of obtaining typical outcomes.

• Consensus Building:

Take a stab at agreement instead of forcing choices. Participate in cooperative dynamic cycles that permit the two players to feel responsibility for conclusive understanding, building up responsibility and collaboration.

• Flexibility and Adaptability:

Keep up with adaptability and flexibility all through the exchange. The ability to change techniques considering emerging information or changing components adds to a more special and responsive negotiation process.

With a focus on working with effort, creativity, and the production of gigantic worth for all parties, arbiters can examine the intricacies of the negotiation scene by using these procedures. The goal is to develop an environment where the different sides feel content with the outcomes, at last inciting a regularly supportive comprehension.

The importance of closing negotiations on a positive note

Shutting dealings ideally holds monstrous significance as it spreads out the energy for the post-negotiation relationship and adds to the overall headway of the perception. Since they host an enduring effect on the two gatherings, the last phases of a negotiation are essential. A positive determination makes a feeling of fulfillment and generosity, encouraging a productive climate that stretches out past the negotiation room.

One key aspect of closing on a positive note is the reinforcement of mutual respect. Communicating appreciation for the other party's commitments and endeavors shows an acknowledgment of their worth in the negotiation. This affirmation assists with facilitating any waiting strains and lays out the establishment for a productive relationship following negotiation.

Besides, a positive end adds to the support of trust between coordinating gatherings. Trust is an essential part in any productive relationship, and the last previews of a conversation present a significant opportunity to develop this trust. At the point when the two players feel regarded and esteemed, they are bound to move toward future connections with receptiveness and a readiness to team up.

Closing on a positive note also aids in securing commitment to the finalized agreement. When both parties leave the negotiation feeling satisfied and appreciated, there is a greater likelihood of honoring the terms of the agreement. This positive feeling goes about as an inspiration for the two players to maintain their part of the deal and work towards the fruitful execution of the arranged terms

The psychological impact of a positive conclusion should not be underestimated. People are impacted by feelings, and the manner in which a negotiation closes can have an enduring effect on people. By finishing up optimistically, negotiators improve the general insight for all gatherings by adding to a feeling of achievement.

Having a positive conclusion after negotiation also adds to the general standing of the gatherings in question. Verbal exchange and expert organizations assume a significant part in business cooperations. A positive outcome increases the likelihood of positive suggestions and references, establishing a favorable reputation for future negotiations.

The significance of shutting exchanges optimistically goes past the prompt fulfillment of the ongoing arrangement. It makes way for a positive post-discussion relationship, reinforces common regard and trust, ties down obligation to the understanding, and adds to an ideal expert standing. As moderators take a stab at mutual benefit results, guaranteeing a positive conclusion is a critical part of making enduring progress in the discussion process.

Reflecting on the negotiation process and learning from experiences

A major piece of expert new turn of events and persevering improvement is thinking about the negotiation participation and securing from encounters. It facilitates a shrewdness assessment of the perspective utilized, the bits of the discussion, and the results accomplished. Here are key pieces of the reflective process:

• Analyzing Strategies:

Start by examining the strategies utilized during the conversation. Study the sensibility of your system, taking into account both convincing viewpoints and regions that could require refinement. Take into consideration how well your systems distinguish your primary objectives and targets.

• Identifying Strengths and Weaknesses:

Identify your strengths and weaknesses as a negotiator. Acknowledge the skills and techniques that contributed positively to the negotiation, and equally, recognize areas where improvement is possible. Genuine self-evaluation is fundamental for development.

• Assessing Communication:

Evaluate the effectiveness of communication throughout the negotiation. Consider how well you conveyed your messages, actively listened to the other party, and adapted your communication style to the dynamics of the negotiation.

• Understanding Dynamics:

Reflect on the interpersonal dynamics at play. Consider what the connection between negotiating parties meant for the cycle. In later negotiations, a more nuanced approach is made conceivable by grasping the elements.

• Examining Decision-Making:

Examine the decision-making process. Evaluate whether choices were made in a calculated manner, in light of an exhaustive thought of needs, and in the event that the decisions lineup with long term targets.

• Reviewing Adaptability:

Reflect on your adaptability during the negotiation. Also consider how well you adjusted strategies in response to changing circumstances or unexpected developments. Flexibility is a basic quality in convincing negotiators.

• Identifying Lessons Learned:

Identify specific lessons learned from the negotiation. Think about what functioned admirably, what might have been taken care of in an unexpected way, and the bits of knowledge acquired from the whole experience.These examples are helpful data for future negotiations.

• Soliciting Feedback:

If applicable, solicit feedback from others involved in the negotiation. Contribution from colleagues or outside eyewitnesses can give extra points of view and significant bits of knowledge that may not be promptly evident.

• Implementing Changes:

Based on the reflections and lessons learned, implement changes to your negotiation approach. This could include refining explicit systems, upgrading relational abilities, or taking on new strategies that line up with your advancing comprehension of viable negotiation.

• Continuous Improvement:

Embrace a mindset of continuous improvement. Perceive that every exchange is a learning, a valuable open door, and a pledge to continuous development as a mediator positions you for outcome in ongoing undertakings.

By effectively captivating in the reflective process, negotiators upgrade their own abilities as well as add to the progression of the more extensive field of negotiation. The capacity to gain from encounters and apply bits of knowledge acquired guarantees that every negotiation turns into a venturing stone toward more noteworthy mastery and outcome in the craft of negotiation.

Conclusion

All in all, "Negotiating for Beginners 2024" has been created as an available and engaging aid for those wandering into the unpredictable universe of exchange. All through these pages, we've explored the intricacies of the exchange scene, underlining lucidity, flexibility, and the improvement of basic abilities.

As beginners retain the standards of successful correspondence, the meaning of figuring out the elements of negotiation, and the craft of settling on some shared interest, they leave on a groundbreaking excursion. The significance of shutting negotiation optimistically has been highlighted, perceiving its effect on building trust and making way for future fruitful corporations.

As well as showing fledglings the basics of discussion, this book plans to impart in them an outlook of continuous learning and improvement. We see each and every negotiation, no matter how big or small, as a great opportunity to learn. Readers are able to move toward dealings with newly discovered certainty and vital keenness thanks to the experiences that are shared within these pages, which serve as stepping stones.

As beginners reflect on the principles outlined in "Negotiating for Beginners 2024," they are invited to recognize negotiation not merely as a skill to be acquired but as an ongoing and evolving process.The objective is to enable perusers to explore talks with lucidity, participate in viable correspondence, and eventually accomplish results that line up with their goals.

May this guide be a believed ally for beginners as they set out on their discussion processes. May it motivate a feeling of interest, strength, and a guarantee to nonstop improvement. Negotiation is, all things considered, an expertise that can be sharpened over the long term, and with every negotiation, negotiators have the chance to refine their methodology and excel at the same time.

Review page

Dear Reader,

I trust this message finds you well. I am reaching out to express my gratitude for choosing to read "Negotiating for Beginners 2024." I genuinely value your opinion and would greatly appreciate it if you could take a moment to share your thoughts and opinion by leaving a review.

Your feedback is extremely helpful in determining the book's future direction and providing other potential readers with insights. Whether you found the content insightful, have suggestions for improvement, or wish to share how the book has impacted you, your perspective is highly valued.

To leave a review, if it's not too much trouble, visit the Amazon platform.Your honest review won't just help me in refining my work yet additionally assist fellow readers make informed decisions.

Much obliged to you for being a piece of this excursion, and I anticipate hearing your thoughts.

Best regards,

Daryl V. Meyer

Author of "Negotiating for Beginners 2024"

www.ingramcontent.com/pod-product-compliance
Lightning Source LLC
Chambersburg PA
CBHW072203290526
45794CB00004B/1626